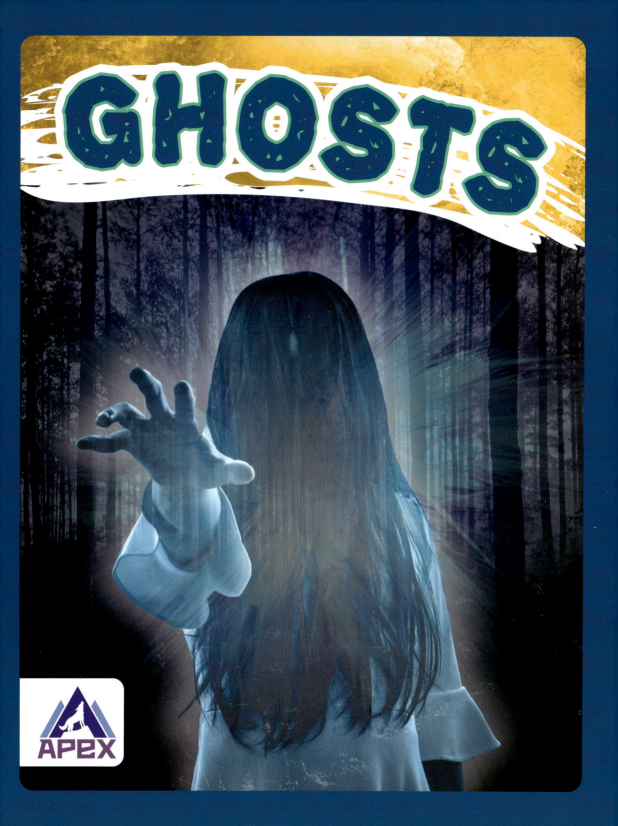

WWW.APEXEDITIONS.COM

Copyright © 2022 by Apex Editions, Mendota Heights, MN 55120. All rights reserved. No part of this book may be reproduced or utilized in any form or by any means without written permission from the publisher.

Apex is distributed by North Star Editions:
sales@northstareditions.com | 888-417-0195

Produced for Apex by Red Line Editorial.

Photographs ©: Shutterstock Images, cover (ghost), 1 (ghost), 4–5, 6, 7, 8–9, 10–11, 12–13, 14, 16–17, 18, 19, 20, 21, 24–25, 26–27, 29; Unsplash, cover (background), 1 (background); iStockphoto, 15, 22–23

Library of Congress Control Number: 2021915676

ISBN
978-1-63738-162-5 (hardcover)
978-1-63738-198-4 (paperback)
978-1-63738-267-7 (ebook pdf)
978-1-63738-234-9 (hosted ebook)

Printed in the United States of America
Mankato, MN
012022

NOTE TO PARENTS AND EDUCATORS

Apex books are designed to build literacy skills in striving readers. Exciting, high-interest content attracts and holds readers' attention. The text is carefully leveled to allow students to achieve success quickly. Additional features, such as bolded glossary words for difficult terms, help build comprehension.

TABLE OF CONTENTS

CHAPTER 1
A GHOST STORY 5

CHAPTER 2
WHAT ARE GHOSTS? 11

CHAPTER 3
GHOSTLY HISTORY 17

CHAPTER 4
EXPLANATIONS 23

Comprehension Questions • 28

Glossary • 30

To Learn More • 31

About the Author • 31

Index • 32

CHAPTER 1

A GHOST STORY

A girl wakes in the middle of the night. Her room is dark and quiet. But something catches her eye.

Many ghost sightings take place at night.

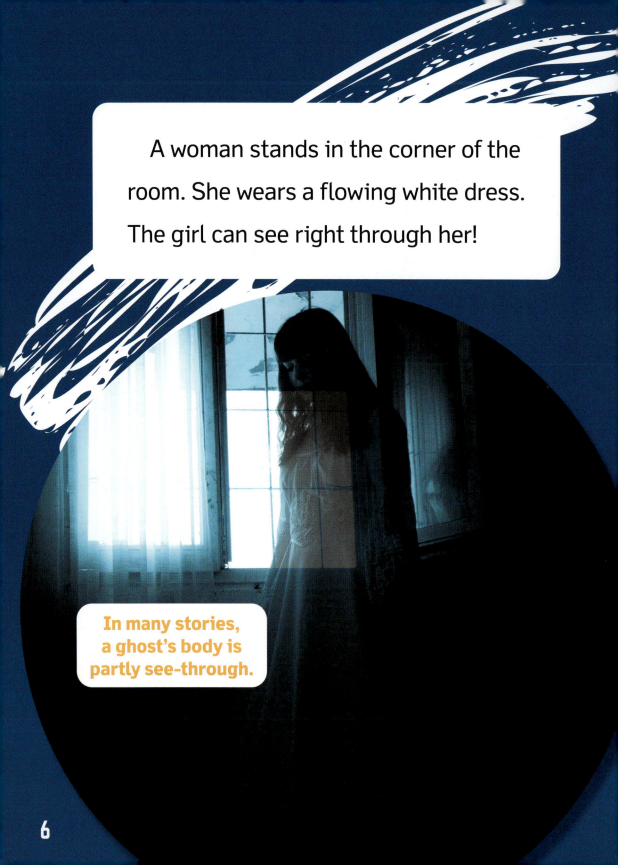

A woman stands in the corner of the room. She wears a flowing white dress. The girl can see right through her!

In many stories, a ghost's body is partly see-through.

La Llorona is a ghost from Latin American folktales. Stories describe her as a skeleton in a white dress.

LA LLORONA

Ghosts often wear white clothes. One famous example is La Llorona. This ghost appears near water. She cries for her children, who drowned. Her name means "weeping woman."

The girl turns on a light. The woman is gone. The girl's heart pounds. Has she seen a ghost? Or was it just her **imagination**?

About one in five people say they have seen or felt a ghost.

Common signs of ghosts include unexplained lights and sounds.

CHAPTER 2
WHAT ARE GHOSTS?

A ghost is the spirit of someone who has died. There are many types of ghosts. Some look like people or animals. Others appear as strange lights or fog.

For many years, people were buried in white sheets. Ghosts are often shown wearing them.

However, not all ghosts can be seen. Some ghosts make rooms feel cold. Some ghosts cause strange sounds. Others cause bad smells.

POLTERGEISTS

Poltergeists can make noise and move objects. These ghosts are **invisible**. But they cause problems. They may throw or break things. They may even hit or pinch people.

Poltergeists may haunt people's homes. These ghosts can make objects move or shake.

Some types of ghosts rattle or tap walls or doors. A few ghosts can even touch or talk to people.

In some ghost stories, people feel a cold hand touch their shoulders.

People have claimed to hear ghosts whisper, scream, laugh, and moan.

When pets stare at empty corners, some people claim they see ghosts.

CHAPTER 3
GHOSTLY HISTORY

People have told ghost stories since long ago. In many stories, ghosts can't move on to the **afterlife**. Some ghosts roam the earth. Others haunt certain places.

Some ghosts are trapped on Earth. Others don't want to go to the afterlife.

For example, many ghosts return to places they lived or died. Some ghosts want **revenge**. But not all ghosts are dangerous.

President Abraham Lincoln was shot in 1865. Some White House visitors claim to see his ghost.

The Tower of London is said to be one of the most haunted places in England.

PAST PRISONERS

The Tower of London is more than 900 years old. Many prisoners have been kept there. Some of their ghosts are said to walk the tower's halls. One guard even reported seeing a ghost bear!

Some people try to find or talk to ghosts. They use cameras, **sensors**, and other tools. They look for signs of hauntings.

Ghost-hunting tools help people record images, sounds, temperature, and more.

Many stories claim ghosts can affect electromagnetic fields (EMFs).

CHAPTER 4
EXPLANATIONS

Some ghost stories are made up to trick or scare people. But other people really do see and hear strange things. There are several possible reasons.

People can combine two photos to make it look like there is a ghost.

Some buildings have mold or poisonous gases. Breathing these **substances** can make people **hallucinate**.

Strong EMFs can make people feel dizzy or see flashes of light.

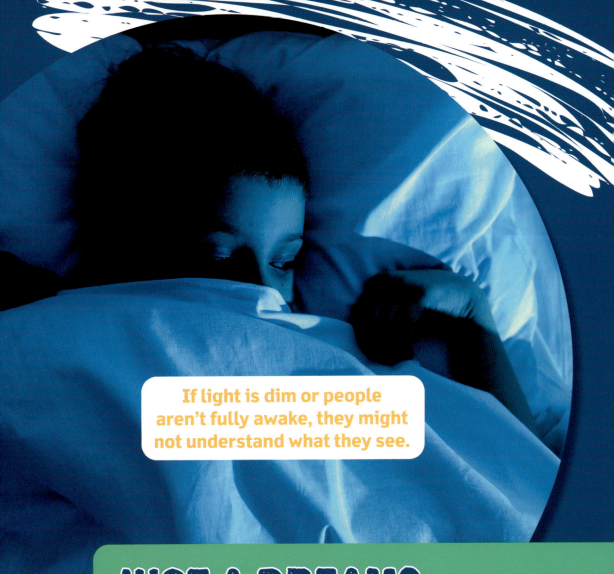

If light is dim or people aren't fully awake, they might not understand what they see.

JUST A DREAM?

While people sleep, their bodies are **paralyzed**. Sometimes, people don't wake up fully. They still can't move. They may see scary shadows. Or they may feel like something is choking them.

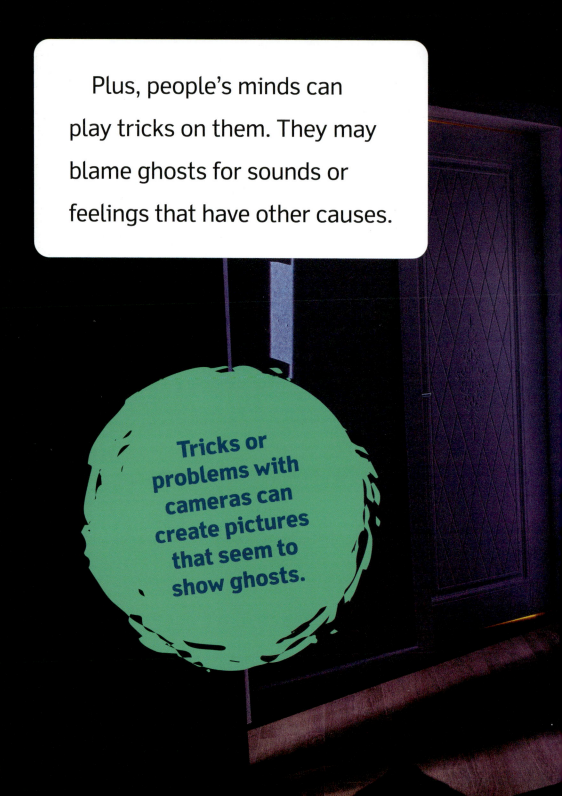

Plus, people's minds can play tricks on them. They may blame ghosts for sounds or feelings that have other causes.

Tricks or problems with cameras can create pictures that seem to show ghosts.

Floating lights or shadows appear in some pictures. Some people believe they are ghosts.

COMPREHENSION QUESTIONS

Write your answers on a separate piece of paper.

1. Write a sentence explaining one scientific reason a person might see a ghost.

2. Do you enjoy reading or hearing ghost stories? Why or why not?

3. According to legend, where do many ghosts appear?

    A. in bright, sunny places
    B. in places they lived or died
    C. in places with no people

4. Which action might a poltergeist do?

    A. throw a chair across a room
    B. take the shape of a dog
    C. take the shape of a person

5. What does **roam** mean in this book?

Some ghosts roam the earth. Others haunt certain places.

- **A.** to move throughout a large area
- **B.** to stay in one small place
- **C.** to not do anything

6. What does **reported** mean in this book?

Some of their ghosts are said to walk the tower's halls. One guard even reported seeing a ghost bear!

- **A.** woke up late
- **B.** read a book
- **C.** told about something seen or heard

Answer key on page 32.

GLOSSARY

afterlife
A place some people believe spirits go after death.

electromagnetic fields
Areas of forces given off by power lines, appliances, and other items that use electricity.

hallucinate
To see, hear, or feel something that seems real but doesn't actually exist.

imagination
A person's ability to make up or invent things.

invisible
Not able to be seen.

paralyzed
Not able to move.

revenge
Getting back at someone who has caused hurt or anger.

sensors
Tools that take in information, such as sounds or movement.

substances
Different kinds of materials, including solids, liquids, and gases.

TO LEARN MORE

BOOKS
Abdo, Kenny. *Ghosts*. Minneapolis: Abdo Publishing, 2020.
Morrison, Marie. *The Tower of London Is Haunted!* New York: PowerKids Press, 2020.
Peterson, Megan Cooley. *Strange Sights in the White House and Other Hauntings in Washington, D.C.* North Mankato, MN: Capstone Press, 2021.

ONLINE RESOURCES
Visit **www.apexeditions.com** to find links and resources related to this title.

ABOUT THE AUTHOR

Lily Loye has been an editor and children's book author for more than 20 years. She loves all things scary, spooky, and creepy but has never seen a ghost herself. She lives in Mankato, Minnesota, with her family, plus two dogs, one cat, and a cuddly bearded dragon.

INDEX

A
afterlife, 17
animals, 11, 19

C
cameras, 20, 26

E
electromagnetic fields (EMFs), 21, 24

F
feelings, 12, 24–26
fog, 11

G
gases, 24

H
hallucinate, 24
haunting, 17, 20

L
La Llorona, 7
lights, 8, 11, 24

M
mold, 24

P
poltergeists, 12

S
sensors, 20
smells, 12
sounds, 12, 14, 26
spirits, 11

T
Tower of London, 19

Answer Key:
1. Answers will vary; **2.** Answers will vary; **3.** B; **4.** A; **5.** A; **6.** C